TIGHTROPE WRITING

Poems by Speak Out Loud Members
Presented by Harvard College Speak Out Loud
November 2013

Written by
Harvard College Student Poets
Published by
Harvard College Speak Out Loud
www.hcs.harvard.edu/speakoutloud/

Copyright © 2013 Harvard College Speak Out Loud
ISBN-13: 978-1493537525
ISBN-10: 1493537520

Printed in the United States of America

TABLE OF CONTENTS

PREGAME

fellow soul,
we will box the long shadows of overworked mornings and sleepy dusks,
      wrap knuckles, tuck thumbs under fingers, the corporeal lives
today.
we will pucker up and kiss those booboos, worries, and stresses away,
      watch them flutter out the window, let them leave as ghostly as
they came.
we will party tonight … either in pajamas or in our sunday (or friday)
finest.
so pray to your God, to the Universe, to your friends that you will
remember this night,
turn up the volume and send your neighbors a blast of the playlist your
tongue has memorized,
find that contour-hugging outfit that snugly fits you and your riveting
confidence in its seams.
we will gather old farts and new faces and
talk until the sun peaks from its forever blanket, rises to scold us.

so you ask me, love, how will we do all this?

i tell you have already begun by cracking this spine.
what lies in your lap is moments of love. this is for the nights you are
losing balance.
when your lifelines are growing thin and weary.
when you need a net to meet your face plant with open spindly arms.
when mary poppins' umbrella would definitely come in handy.
when the edge came up too suddenly and you're waiting for something
to pull you back.

this is for the days when balance is restored.
when lady justice has finally kicked off her heels from the night before.
when karma finally found its keys.
when friends finally compliment your new 'do.

my love,
this is for the moments when you're tipping on life's fine line.

just look behind you.
we, the tightrope writers, hold out our hands.
let's line-dance.

DEAR BODY, BY JAMIE BANKS

This is my first confession.

I am sorry:
I have never known how to love you.
I do know it's not a matter of those words on my tongue--
The tongue is our strongest muscle, but
My words can't lift you.

Forgive me--for once being too young to distinguish kindnesses and violences.
I made a promise to lie about your bruises with a promise-breaking man
I'm sorry I kept the covenant—
For flying the airplane toy chest he always swore he'd make me all the way to silence.

I have really
No
Sometimes
Tried to treat you well.
You'll remember my rosary:
"Take care of yourself so you're strong enough to fight"
"Consider the temple of the body"--uttered as a missionary's message from the mind.
"Smart people are strong enough not to be fat:
So are you not smart or not a person?"

I promise I will never again take weight as a matter of character.

Pardon me while I re-learn myself.
I am learning my colors again:
Then there was blood red, puke green, black blue with rings of healing yellow
Now I know about the shading of the air
Off-medication disoriented, adrenaline electric, depression dull, love-full wisp-of-breath.

I know you only speak chemicals. I thought I'd get through to you still.
See,
Pain
Is my native language.
I thought we could share it.
I sent you down messages as pills in a bottle
More, in my life, than the average
Drug addict.
I know "getting better" means a room full of feeding tubes.

I can only talk shit in chemicals. I've--
Withheld serotonin
Refused you the morphine,
And shot up daily doses of dopamine.

I've let other people talk shit to you too.
But let me tell you how I hear what they say.
'Cause, really?
Scarface is a pretty badass nickname.

It's time you know that I've opened negotiations with a few of your
constituents.

Your scars I trace at night, like caressing—

To your hands—my hands.
You sometimes flap too much
But you are the only ones for me
I even think you're kind of cute sometimes
And I have once looked down at you after a long day's heavy work, and
thought
"These alone will get me through."

To my voice, for occasionally initiating a heart-to-heart miracle—
Thank you. I love you.

I have reported all my ailments to the Department of Health and Mental
Hygiene
But I've brushed my brain twice a day for years
And there is still a lot of plaque.

But never mind that.
My hands, my voice:
I'll sing you the instructions and you build me the body.
If you'll clean up the temple, I'll make it a home again.
I promise to pay the rent and clean the bathroom.
I want open spaces, lots of windows—
As an atypical guy, I've even read the manual and I
Got the theory
Down.

It's time to practice, love.
Dance with me.

Jamie Banks, Class of 2013

Jamie likes people, words, and mental health, and especially combining those through teaching.

GEOFFREY, BY MELANIE WANG

geoffrey the giant is born in a blizzard. while snow piles gargantuan,
oxygen whoomps into his lungs.
the nurse pronounces him a boy, and nothing seems suspect,
not until later, when mum and dad realize that they can measure their
baby lengthening in inches per week.

geoffrey grows. seems to get more out of his mushed peas your average
infant, but
doctors can never name one thing wrong. stethoscope-cold and kindly
they ask how much he eats and how much he shits and how much he
cries.
but there are no easy answers for why a body might too much for a boy,
or, why a boy might be too much for his body.
does his soul scratch at the soles of his feet and implore his legs to grow
longer?
are there weights that pull at the tips of his fingers, or a god that is
stretching his spine?
does he want to be bigger than he is?

by the time he starts walking geoffrey is too much for a crib,
his parents buy a king bed but can't find the dinosaur sheets he asks for,
not in that size.
this is only the beginning: next, the kindergarten teacher
that thinks one day about reading jack and the beanstalk during
storytime before she catches herself

geoffrey is smart and moves quick through chapter books
though they are always overwhelmed in his grasping dinner plate hands.
by fifth grade, he is seven feet tall,
his mother dresses him in bright striped shirts, jeans, reeboks,
dreads the day he is too big to wear anything you can buy in a store,
always hopes her eleven-year-old won't be mistaken for a man.

the cruelest kids slip notes in his backpack
that read *fee fi fo fum*
until he starts humming it at recess
just to screw with 'em.
he takes to memorizing capitals -
the capital of hungary is budapest.
the capital of vietnam is hanoi,

the capital of mongolia is ulaanbaatar.

his first kiss is named molly. she plays violin, has a heart like lion,
and it happened on her porch steps while her father sat panicked inside.
*you're telling me you want to date a giant? a boy who could literally
crush you?*
later she tells him it was sweet but too strange to continue
and geoffrey thinks to himself *who in this situation is crushed, really?*

at graduation, he is taller than two principal huxleys.
that summer he works at the lake as a lifeguard - gets there early in the
morning
to do long laps across its lengths, back and forth.
darkens until he is tan like the color of good clay.

geoffrey is seventeen years, twelve foot and still growing,
doesn't fit in the house quite the same,
can't find a bed that suits him,
takes to sleeping on two mattresses laid across his bedroom floor.

in his dreams, he is finally giant enough to get a bird's-eye view of this
town.
he can watch his mother's sedan sputter to work in the mornings,
can watch pedestrians sliding like water droplets across these streets.

geoffrey dreams he is tiptoeing through green backyards, so as not to
damage any roofs.
he dreams he is finally walking out of this place.
he dreams there is someplace big enough for him to go.

Melanie Wang, Class of 2015

Melanie Wang is currently a Social Studies and WGS concentrator living
in Eliot. She is always a woman/writer/student and getting weirder all the
time.

THE ACT OF LETTING GO, BY KAT BAUS

Think about the first brush of your lips,
of his soft smile when you opened to him, cereus,
remember the way he looked at you
and mouthed your name like a supplication
or thanks. How his fingers basketwoven in yours
pinched the ring on your middle finger.
Decide to allow yourself to forget.

Help him seal into boxes with packing tape
the room you shared at the end of the semester.
Gather the emptied cups of honeyed tea,
the peppermint wrappers, the expensive vodka
you ran out of time to drink, your drafts
with corners curled nestlike on his bottom shelf.
Throw them away.

Ask him to make love to you one more time
and understand when he tells you that he can't.
Lie with him on the stripped mattress
and trace the ghosts of posters beside the bed,
the cathedral, the old guitarist.
Collect your earrings from the nightstand.
Put them on.

Tell him goodbye at the post office
where you drag his suitcases like casualties by their ankles.
Goodbye on the street corner outside your dorm,
across from the ageing cemetery, eyes shut
against his shoulder and the windworn names.
In three months, watch him shut the door of a white SUV
with wilted flowers in the cupholder.

Understand that you will never return to this place.
Make a map of its geography and rest it in the end-pages of loved books.
Understand that you will never have said goodbye enough.
Understand that you will always want another night sweetened
with still bodies and the breath of opened flowers.
Understand that writing poems, like this one,
will not make him your lover again.

You will begin by writing poems to him
and reading them aloud with your eyes low on the page.
You will think about suicide
and wonder whether the act of letting go
is the same as admitting that something has already died
or opening your palms so it can sigh away

and wonder which of these is a greater loss.

Keep writing poems. Write poems that make you cry
because each time you twist off the plastic cap
the carbonation of your pain will escape a little.
In time, he will become apostrophe.
In time you will find another second person,
remember there are other readers, and you.
Write poems about him until you have made him a fiction.

Tonight, put on makeup, dab sandalwood perfume
behind your ears, slip on the black silk panties
the ones embroidered with pink blossoms
and with the satin bow at the waist
understanding that no one will see them but you.
Step outside with your hands and your poems
folded in your coat pockets,

and you will see someone you might have known
once, and take your hand from your pocket
and feel an odd flutter, and smile at them, and wave
with the cold lapping at your palm
and keep walking
and forget to look for the papers
waving back at you, white, across the snow.

---

kat baus, Class of 2015

kat baus is a New Orleans native; queer organizer; director; designer;
model; poet; playwright; fiction-, nonfiction-, & metafiction-writer; &
aspiring BA in English at Harvard College '15.

UNDERGROUND, BY SOFIA ESCUDERO

These days I've gotten pretty good at melting
because sometimes my feet prefer being covered in leaves
instead of socks
and once your toes start to spread into the earth
it's not such a stretch for the rest of your bones
to soften the marrow into foam
let fingernails be pebbles, and lungs turn to loam
winding down through the topsoil
filters the cobwebs from my capillaries
because I've hugged plenty of trees but never the roots
never washed my face with last week's rain
and sometimes being seen is enough to dry me out
and the only way to quench my palms
is to soak in an aquifer.

Slipping down through the earth
is like diving in slow motion.
My heels dig deep because there's enough dirt down there
to swaddle me, keep my biceps in my arms
and my head away from harm.
Melting is the safest
because you can't break hot wax
you can look for your ax but I won't be your firewood,
and it feels so good
to let the pine needles knit a blanket over my head
no, I don't want to be dead
just unbroken.

The flames at the back of my throat ache to be put out,
I let my body slip down
next to earthworms and other travellers
because underground, my calves are light like jellyfish.
My ears feel vibrations, not sounds
and sometimes the world up here is too damn loud.
Deep down there's no shrieking wind to ask
why my lips are all alone,
nowhere for my tears to be blown, my fears I can own
when I'm under the earth they don't sting me like nettles
they just sink with me.
Let me be.

I promise I'll come up again,
just don't ask me when.
I'll find a lake.
Stitch myself together under the algae
brush the mud from my collarbones

---

minnows tickling my ankles,
relearning my elbows,
unsticking my eyelashes and letting my lungs float,
loosing my tongue so I can tell you
that the memory of your skin is still on my hands
like a second set of fingerprints
because even after all the melting and sliding,
not hiding, just healing,
you've stayed in my head.

When my forehead breaks the surface
I'll accept the air's kiss
rub shoulders with birdsong
let the wind's fingers whisper across my face
because I needed to melt myself down and start again
let go of my dead leaves and
rest my head on bedrock,
scrub the scabs from my heartstrings and grip tree roots like pens

But I've missed the air,
I want stars in my hair
and clouds on my fingertips,
and I'm ready for sky again.

Sofia Escudero, Class of 2016

Sofia is right now probably either reading a book or eating a
pomegranate. She likes drinking tea on cold days, ideally with company.

MONA LISA SMILE, BY OLUWASEUN ANIMASHAUN

Lisa laughed and danced,
Lisa laughed and danced because that's what all the young girls do
She paraded, posed and was captured by a man that no one quite knew
but he would uplift her famous with a single image,
and she,
she will always have her body pressed within his sheets

he placed her in between the frames of his bed
he was trying to depict love with strokes that were nothing but forced
nature could not quite mix paint the way he could,
all he needed to do was add a little more
just. a. bit. more.

he slid his fingers back and forth,
getting a feel for his canvas ...
its texture, its length, how far he can stretch its limbs

he painted her as best as he could - with a deep secret that no one could
ever reach
his blank mind filling with images,
imagining a Lisa who enjoyed this secret
she could only hold still

he sketched across her body love in blue and purple violets that bloomed
against the spring of her skin
but the picture was not quite right yet,
he needed some green and red
so he opened green veins and poured deep crimson,
now she was complimented the proper foreground

the final touch -
a teeth-gritted smile to imprison the night's memories
set permanently in the rigor mortis of Lisa's twilight

her eyes followed him as they lolled lifelessly
and her eyes followed him as he walked away from his masterpiece
and her eyes followed him

Oluwaseun Animashaun, Class of 2014

Oluwaseun Animashaun, affectionately known as Olu, loves to laugh
uproariously, dance in the sunlight, and teach little roses in the concrete
jungle.

FURNACE, BY VIRGINIA MARSHALL

Your father is a furnace,
My mother said to me.
There are cracks in every sidewalk,
And the streetlights yawn toward the asphalt
It is winter where we are.

I am furnace-less, but my bed
Is pushed up next to a radiator
And when I wake up to the stars
Screaming, sometimes I hit my eyebrow
On the radiator, unintentionally.
Tonight, the bump on my forehead pulses
Like nobody's mother;
I don't put on make-up anymore.

At nights, the leaves scramble
And I pile on blanket after blanket
Like a several surreptitious hugs.
I'm lacking my own personal furnace,
I've only got a body brilliant, a radiator,
And a mother far away.

I'm learning how to keep flowers alive,
Like Mrs. Dalloway and her brilliant pep,
"How do you feel about cut flowers?"
I ask my radiator,
Who is standing in for the furnace.
He just purrs and says,
"beautiful, like incredibly so."
I don't correct his grammar,
Only roll over and think about
My home furnace, though it is gone now
And the ticking-settling-in noises
It must make at night.

I write home, sometimes,
Drafting the prose line by line,
Windows closed to keep out the chilly draft:
Dear furnace father,
Keep my mother warm, and
Make friends with the thermostat,
I'll cover the heating costs from afar.
It's chilly in this bombed-out city
Nights covered in insulation,
This smog we've grown around our
Sweating arm-pits.

Dear daughter,
My home-furnace writes back—
Forget not the cut flowers I spilled
Off the breakfast tray.
Put them in water, stems diagonally cut,
And give them some sun.

Dear God, Son, Holy Heater,
Remember my wit and my fortitude
Tell all the warm bodies to kiss
The brilliant ones, until it is possible
To forget all these folds of skin.
Wake this weighted, warped city at five-thirty
With whistling air-raids.

Dear me, oh my,
Remind my tripping heart
To tick on time. Everyone needs
Her own personal furnace and a solid set of mantras
If it was meant to be, it will, I tell
My radiator. *Making a bed keeps
The mattress monsters away.*

Oh furnished furnace, mantra me to distraction
*This too shall pass,
To each his own,
Brush the backs of your teeth as well as the fronts.*
Keep the furnace far from your head
At night, but let the street lights in,
Let those orange illuminators yawn you to sleep,
Let them grace your steaming temples;
Your own personal body brilliant.

Virginia Marshall, Class of 2015

Virginia goes by Ginger most of the time, finds her freckles to be
frustrating, and decorated her room with wall decals of birds.

SABRA'S SANDBOX, BY MARIAH BROWNE & SASANKA JINADASA

weightless, she took
too many steps forward
and forgot that she was
poison

yearning is an act of romance for the pure
but destruction in her palms
she held a black widow and it spun
threads around her ring finger and cried so lightly
she thought her palms were sweating
moist enough at last
to greet her daughter's cheeks
without splintering silken flesh

she held that ring of spun silk until
it yellowed gracefully and Sabra
let her make excuses
night after night
nestled in sandpaper hope

after too many steps forward
she slipped through the ring
to land in her daughter's dimples
took a bite
swallowed her in blistering nostalgia
branded her skin with apologetic kisses

becoming weightless like her mother
Sabra demanded the wind paint the night with her ashes
forgetting that she
was now poison too

Mariah Browne, Class of 2015

Mariah Browne, eats cereal for dinner and chocolate for breakfast.
Regrets nothing.

Sasanka Jinadasa, Class of 2015

Sasanka is a queer South Asian woman decolonizing histories,
destabilizing the patriarchy, and destroying casual racists in her gender
studies classes. Equity > equality.

you are now free
            to roam about
        the pages.

                                    it's 10 o'clock
                                do you know where
                                    your mind is?

let your eyes glaze over the words.

            drink   (the meanings)   responsibly.

we
are not
accountable
for the morning after
(but we do agree with the
actions of the night before.)

INTERMISSION

                            any resemblance to real person, living
                                or dead, is purely coincidental…
                                        except when not.

all opinions expressed are 99.49% true.

                                        answer emails
                                from foreign princes
                        and all your royalties will disappear.

            only YOU can (create) wildfires.

one does not
        simply walk
                into mordor…
    you have to stroll in with a crew.

                            don't
                                step on
                                        the
                                            mome raths.
if you see something,
            WRITE something.

EXPOSE, BY BRIDGET IRVINE

"everything you feel is justified."
okay. i shrug my shoulder from your hand.
counterargument: what about my friends who apologize for all that they
say?
i'm sorry. that wasn't 100% honest actually.
my friends do it, yes, but i am just as sorry.
we quote lyrics at you, to gold-plate our insecurities
but is that justified,
that sorrow for consciousness?
[*i'm sorry i'm sorry i'm s o r r y*]
i admit it - we are serial apologizers
(though not *apologists,* there's nothing defensive going on here—)
or is there?
in that immediate absolution from responsibility?
i admit it
but i'm trying to doubt it
sowing doubt in soil
i want to doubt my remorse more than I doubt meaning
i want its feet cut out from under it - a child in the sea
i want those near me not to <u>feel</u> "justified"
(which implies a sort of subjective piecemeal judgment system)
but to <u>live</u> in a static-yet-active body of water
floating – okay.
i.e. you are not a black spot nor a nuisance nor a non-person
but just as ready to sing as the next woman.
so. since we're talking about feelings for once.
the silicate center of the earth, if exposed, would not survive as is
seismic waves whisper that the crystals in the inner core have aligned
themselves into one big crystal
- geologists take heed, because even though we know it's there
we cannot observe nor collect it, this meaty stony warmth
if the core were split
its pressure would vanish
and the center would melt, flash-quick.
so maybe one way we can *feel*
is by leaving the center be.

i don't mean down w/ all mental inactivity though to be clear!
because i can hear your minds whirring and whispering that beautiful
"wait—"
(good.)
i think we can still observe!
like
one night i was thinking in that pre-sleep depth
and i felt my heart beat (what a *trope*)
i tried to feel w/ my tongue how that beat *was*

you know like – "babump" or "ththump"
but those words are limited (i love limits)

so i wondered -
what about that gap?
between my heard heart through the pillow
and the heart that sometimes fills and empties? flash-quick.
well. i've learned that irony exploits the gaps between what *is* and *is not*
said
i'd like you to exploit the gap between what actually *is* and *is not* in this
world.
appropriated idea: examining moments of positivity
- - dissecting the crystallized core of the heart - -
is soul deadening.
whereas describing negativity & pain freezes it into one solid block to
fling at the ground,
the surface of the earth.
i'm done. but here—
idea: keep your heart molten and your head liquid.

Bridget Irvine, Class of 2016

Bridget is not a poet; her words are often just hands extended into the
semi-darkness that is consciousness. She loves time and conversations
and the musician Sufjan Stevens. All the rest is mystery.

CARNIVAL NOISE, BY DANNY WOOD

It is what it is.
The truth is always the simplest and most obvious conclusion
Fuck the transformers, it's not more than meets the eye

Life's a carnival
A wondrous, beautiful place full of eye-popping attractions

Come One Come All! Feast Your Eyes!
Come see the strong man, the trapeze artist, the contorting quintuplets,
The bearded lady, The fire eater, The frog man, The knife swallower,
Just 20 tickets!

The carnival stands where honest, hard-working people, opportunity
creators, give us chances to win fabulous, fantastic prizes

Who wants a try, Who wants a try, hey you good sir, you seem like a
winner, wanna win something nice for the misses, Well for just 10 tickets
you get three trys to throw this ball through a hole that's too small for it,
uhh I meant the ball is just way too small for that big hole, the game is
too easy. And if you win, you get your choice of three great prizes, made
with the finest materials we find out back, I mean in the outback, I mean
in France, and made by people we don't feed and keep in cages, I mean
that don't need wages, I mean made by Ronald Regan and Miles Davis,
yeah that's it. So what'll ya say?

Thousands of carnival stands, each one offering more elegant,
prestigious prizes than the last at the mere cost of a few more tickets,
promising a few more trys at these games that, at the very least, are
winnable if not a sure thing. Damn, what a great place.
But there's a noise. What's that noise, it's almost silent, but listen, listen
close and it's there. Can you hear it? A chant: A tune beating onward like
the sound of marching steps of Hitler youth. It's playing the phrase my
11th grade US History teacher use to tell us explained everything, he said
it was the underpinning and major motivation for all acts throughout
human history: Cash is King.

Mr. Moore, why did this empire fall: Cash is King, why did this empire
invade: Cash is King, why did they enslave them: Cash is King, why did
they free them: Cash is King, why did he get assassinated, Cash is King,

Mr. Moore, Why do they lie: Cash is King

Yes, money makes the world go round, but the monetary merry go
round is the only ride we don't see at the carnival. Only stand operators
with enough tickets are given proof of its existence: a chance to see it

Among these, competition is then literally cut throat for a vacated seat. And riding is very dangerous, the money-go-round spins at an amazingly high velocity. Riders perched on their seats must hang on for their lives, as tightly as possible, if they hope to stay on

Getting off and on can be difficult sometimes, even impossible because the money-go-round never stops nor slows down. If one makes it onto a vacated seat intact, a trance will fall over them, even those with the best intentions, for the tune playing on the money-go-round is too seductive, too enchanting not to follow, and soon they too will chant: Cash is King. Cash is King. Cash is King.

No I've never seen this ride, so I can't substantiate my claim with the certainty required by billions who deny it, and the billions used to deny it. I would need proof of it, not mere evidence, well at least I'm told there isn't enough evidence or it isn't good enough. But it is just evidence they need to deny, of which I'm told there is enough. So I guess I'm wrong, I guess there is no money-go-round, surely it doesn't exist, I am clearly misguided, at least I'm told so.

I'm told it is what it is. It's not complex schemes and rides. Rather, the truth is always the simplest and most obvious conclusion.

But why then can I hear the tune. I know stand operators can too, look close enough, and their eyes will betray their secret. That almost silent sound: It is the dog whistle that calls Cerberus to his post, that turns truth-tellers into ghosts; that so many march too, like Hitler youth. Footsteps chanting.

I can't tell you what frequency to turn to in order to hear it clearly. And maybe we don't want to hear it. Enchanted by the fairy tales and bedtime stories we heard as children, maybe we cannot bring ourselves to decode tunes, even of those we choose to hear.

But far beyond claiming the world's clay as their to mold, the money-go-round: it's riders and operators, have accomplished something much more impressive. Being so loud, yet simultaneously so quiet. It is probably better said...

The greatest feat the devil has ever achieved is convincing people he doesn't exist.

Danny Wood, Class of 2014

Enthused by everything, amused by everything, and trying to take in all the world while he is on it. Born in Tampa, Florida. Much Love.

TRUE BEAUTY, BY JALEN T.

Every morning, she does her hair in front a cracked mirror
And whenever a piece falls off, she slowly picks it up and gently puts it back in place
Because this is her perception of beauty

With a mother who left her with nothing but her green eyes at age 2 and a father who died fighting at age 4, at 6 years old, Brianna is now her grandmother's daughter
And on the first day of first grade, she wears ripped jeans and the same shirt she's already worn three times in one week with a book bag over her shoulder holding dull no. 2 pencil, wrinkled paper and some half-eaten crayons
She believes that she has enough but for some reason, the adults around her always ask for more
"Do you wanna take a plate home Brianna?"
Nodding silently, she holds the foil wrapped plate of free food like it was her mother's hand running home to give to her grandmother before it becomes like everything else she's ever owned...broken.

B-R-O-K-I-N is how she chooses to spell it at age 12 because she sees bro for brother and kin for family and wonders if she changes the spelling will it change the meaning its given to her life?
At home, she misses her cracked mirror, but she's now a child of the Robinson family and with them, her book bag always has new pencils, binders and even an iPad
The shirt she used to wear has been replaced with a closet that goes so deep that Brianna is still wearing new clothes
So now the teachers at school always rhetorically say, 'I bet you love your new home, Brianna.'
Nodding silently, she walks home dangling her bookbag on one finger, occasionally dropping it on the ground so that it doesn't look so brand new
On Fridays, when she's allowed to walk home alone, she finds an open field, drops her belongings, rips her sleeves and screams out, 'I hate it here!'
Because she doesn't understand who gave her new home the right to replace her old one and why at every point in her life people always try to fix her because they think she's...broken

The next time she sees the word is in church and upon seeing it, she feels a tear crawling down her cheek as her mind travels back to the room with the cracked mirror
At 16, her new family has went from loving her to complaining that she's too rebellious because she's cracked the mirror in her room several time
However, only she knows that the pieces are her peace

That the cracks of imperfection complete her and whenever a piece falls off, she's reminded of her brokenness
But, as usual, the adults in her life have to ask, 'Why do you like this broken mirror Brianna? What do you see in it?"
But she's grown up enough to answer so she smiles and calmly responds, 'Because brokenness is beautiful.'

Jalem T, Class of 2015

Jalem T has been an aspiring writer since childhood whether by spoken word or novels, constantly inspired by others and his love for Christ.

WITH BRUISED AND CAREFUL HANDS, BY JULIA BECERRA

With bruised and careful hands that I may not be able to grip as tightly
but when so inclined, I find intricacy can be managed, I can avoid
mangling, well, strangling, the toothpaste bottle in the bathroom,
this body of Crest gasping for breath, before it gives off a geyser of its
dream caked cream,
until submitting to its own hygienic death.
Knuckles clamped around toothbrush clasping it like a last lifeline to
keep me from falling back into
hazy dreamscapes, my hands might be worse for wear but at the very
least, they can get my teeth clean.

With bruised and careful hands I can still rub away the nightmares,
from tired eyes—eyes plenty tired but at least not scared anymore,
just aware of the lingering residue of REM rising up from naked irises,
leaking out and away,
my shotty dreams drifting off into the day just more carbon dioxide
to keep the lonely atmosphere company.
Fists clenched are usually meant to meet a face to spark slick pain
but right now mine just want to give my eyes a break;
leave my lids with the seed of alertness and let my vision clarify.

Because my morning brain is still dripping with sleep's hard-gripping
ooze,
yet already taking on the prospective problems
that might take hold of this day—all making my mind
blast thoughts past too fast to grasp with my fingertips but
at least these hands can still carry out the tasks set before them, they can
do what the weary mind can't land a handle on just now and focus.

They don't see what will be;
they take hold of what's there, and they don't care if they've gotten a little
banged up
in rough activity or, weathered by the cold weather, these things aren't
anything new, they're simply
the same elements, that have affected, a sensational amount of
generations of dry and lightly battered hands and I like to think about
the bands of men and women that
travelled the earth before they had anywhere to go—
How did they know the direction their lives would flow?
and when they looked down on bruised and beaten palms
would they acknowledge their blemishes with a shrug and a grunt
no time before the next hunt to be vexed or even register
or would their blisters make them smile a little, give them makeshift
roadmaps of the bite-sized beatings
their fingers had taken in order to achieve their needed goals?
I like to think the latter, not that it matters because

With bruised and powerful hands I think I can still
tie my shoes as tightly as my raft at a harbor, safe for a stay
against storm-sweltered seas of my own nocturnal born insecurities,
because when my soles touch the bottom of my boots
fastened by hands that latch them in with the sureness of
my own daily discovered convictions
I know I'm at least bound by foot to the ground
while my hands are free to fiddle with the rest of the world
pushing off the floor and assembling words together
with the lightest pressure of spiral-printed skin to softly synthetic key.

Julia Becerra, Class of 2016

Julia Becerra is of Midwestern origins, but otherwise hails from the
legendary land of New Jersey. She enjoys reusing jokes until they're no
longer funny.

INCONVENIENCE, BY BXK

I would love to be a convenient transgender person. Easy to sort. Like balling socks of the same, white, color – man, woman, man, oh, oh, hold on, okay, trans man, trans woman. I'd love it.

Yes, I prefer the pronoun 'they' instead of 'he' or 'she'. You're right; 'they' is usually used for plurals. And adapting isn't easy. Like me adapting to the fact that we aren't friends because it's too hard for you to be ungrammatical. She said, "It's already hard enough to tell with Asians, so it's not like you have that going for you."

The convenient trans person is white, young, and sure.
He wears ties and dates women
Been on T since he knew.
She is 'beautiful' enough for you to sign that Miss USA petition, 'sexy' enough that you might get in bed with her even if you weren't getting paid to do it.
I think if you close your eyes, you wouldn't be able to tell.

I'm not denying the pleasure in neatness.
Trust me, I would much rather fall neatly into your binary sock drawers of gender.
I would love to look in my mirror
And see what might be a man
or a white person
or those images of trans people on health brochures that my doctor hands me to teach me about myself.

Even if I collaged a face from those brochures I still wouldn't have the right shade of skin to stop you from looking twice when you card me at the gay bar.

Hell, I wouldn't even have the right shade of skin for you to let me in at a trans people of color event. If you mean black and latino, say so.

"Bex? Does that stand for something?"
"Nope."
"No but what's does it mean?"
"It means me, it's my name."
"No but what did your mother call you?"

If you must know, my mother called me pretty. Never beautiful, never wrote that into a name, never said it out loud, really, only whispered it once when she thought I had fallen asleep on her thigh as she gave me a DIY facial, zits between thumbs style.

I look in the mirror and see how she sees me pretty.

I tie my ties and see it,
flatten my chest, and see it,
and when I finally manage to lose sight of that pretty,
I start to miss my mother's daughter.
See, the gender binary comforts me too.

Twin beds I'll never sleep in, I lay white cotton sheets on them with these hands you call brown because you don't dare say yellow. Sometimes I arrange my body horizontal across them, perfectly still. I'm tired. Hope to God that to the onlooker I pass as a man, or a woman, or… a legitimate trans person, even if just for second. It's not self-hate, only self-preservation. I am always surprised by how comfortable I am with lying like this. I have a hunch that if I close my eyes, you wouldn't be able to tell.

---

bxk, Class of 2013

bxk started writing spoken word a few years ago, and hopes to continue for many more years to come. They also love cooking and napping.

MEASURE THE DISTANCE, BY CASSANDRA EUPHRAT WESTON

The first rule of stage combat
is measure the distance.
Hold out your rapier with your arm stretched taut.
The second rule is measure again
just to be safe. The tip of your weapon
should stop just short of your opponent.

It is convenient to have a cut-off point for tragedy.
The play ends
and the dead bodies rise to bow
or I have seen enough, for today, of far-off glamorous wars
and click closed the tab on my laptop

When we were fourteen my friend Megan was stabbed in a bakery
by a man who had never seen her before
she shouldn't have lived

(if you can afford the best doctors
fate is expendable
prayer is optional
accidents happen
but everything will be okay)

I am *not* okay
with the 131 homicides last year in Oakland, California
I am *outraged*

though I've never actually lived there.

The first rule
is measure the distance. How many steps
in the two blocks from my house
to a doorstep memorial by the 1 California bus stop
measure again
what size is my surprise at this intrusion from--   another
kind of neighborhood.

I believe words like systematic will keep me safe
I believe racism will keep me safe
I believe the fuckery of capitalism will keep me safe

I have never seen a corpse
I can't just click away.
Statistic me that. What percentage of Americans
have never seen a dead body. Raise the stakes.
What percentage of Americans

have never watched somebody die
raise the stakes   what percentage of Americans
have never watched somebody die without warning
and not been surprised

I trust my bones
                not to break my skin

                                not to split

because white skin does not split. Because I have drunk milk at my
parent's insistence for twenty years; now my bones are rich with calcium
and my father's money.
Because I have been taught I can reach what I want
that distance exists to be conquered

I believe I can own this body
despite all evidence to the contrary
I believe it is safe to be alive
despite all evidence to the contrary

Cassandra Euphrat Weston, Class of 2014

Cassandra Euphrat Weston is a word nerd who misses fog and flails her
way toward art and change.

DEAR SON, BY BRYAN ERICKSON

My dear son,
You have not been born yet.
And you might not ever be.
You don't know this yet
But your father is afraid
of his own blood.
He's afraid
Of a lot of things.

My dear son,
I've tried to write these lines
One hundred times
And one hundred times
I've let the words down
And thrown them away.
One hundred times,
I've laid in bed,
Tried to listen to my
Heart beat to a rhythm I've never understood.

I was 5 when
The doctor told my parents
I had a heart murmur.
It's like an off-beat two-step
In my chest,
Right here.
It is a reminder that
my heart is something
not to trust, it's not something
I can own, or belong to.
While I'm curled up in my empty room,
I find my hand is planted over my chest,
waiting for the record to skip again,
hoping I can catch it in time
this time, and
maybe next time
I can be in rhythm
And my heart can teach me the things
My mother never did.

My son,
Don't ask me why I'm afraid to look you in the eye.
I will never tell you,
but I have been afraid of you
ever since you were only
a gossamer flicker

In the back of my head.
You may inherit my shoulders
Or my wide hips
And you may inherit
My sin, the dark shit I try to keep
Tucked in the darker
corners of these lines.
Nobody gives you a guide to life,
But I'm hoping this will be a step forward
After forcing you two steps back.
I hope you don't grow up thinking
You have to be
The strongest one
In the family tree.
My black father didn't want that for me,
nor did his black father before that,
in a long tradition of black fathers
trying to raise their boys stronger than them,
hoping one day
these black backs could be strong enough
to carry the scars of an entire race.
My father taught me
how to read the old scars like a second language,
to see stories and family history
where others see only anguish.

My son,
I hope
You get to fall in love,
make stupid mistakes
live out your life
happy and stupid and
you'll never know what it means
To look at your hands
and know that they do not belong to you anymore.

My son,
I hope you are straight.
I hope you kiss girls,
And you get married
And you get a dog and
You get a house
and you get a mortgage
And you get to argue over taxes
And who snores in bed
With your wife.
You'll never have to grow up with the not-so-old stories
My four fathers told me when I was your age.
The gay friend found beaten half to death,

Shoved in a closet.
The Los Angeles riots in Watts,
Spreading like wildfire screaming "Justice, Justice."
The entire family refusing to look you in the eye after they've told you
they will not have a gay son.
The feeling of fear, that hollow ache in your stomach that keeps
swallowing the words "I'm gay" from coming out.
You'll never know.
I won't tell you.
I refuse to tell you
That you need to suffer to be my son.
You might be born with my shoulders,
You might be born with my brown eyes
And maybe even my mother's wide hips
That remind you that a man who cannot give birth can still create life;
You may have all of the relics of our small family tree,
But you will never
know the pain that seeps deep into the dark, black dirt.

My dear son,
Your father is not always right.
He is not always good.
And if you read this,
I'm sorry, but
Maybe the worst thing I ever did was bring you into a world like this.
Maybe
If I never teach you, never tell you about my family tree,
You'll never notice
Our hearts beat out of sync,
And you'll be ignorant,
But you might be happy.
I will teach you to fight everyone you meet,
To lock up the only gift I have for you –
A tender heart -
To never look back.
Be wary of those feelings that leave you exposed,
Leave you open to growing wounds,
And it might make you stronger.
I hope you believe me
When I lie to you like that.

My son,
I am so sorry
That I ever wished you be born
To someone else,
Someone better than me.
I am so sorry
For ever thinking that
Maybe

if I changed myself enough,
carved out the twisted, fucked up parts of my body
and burned out the gnarled knots and cancers in my bones,
maybe
if I drain enough of my tainted blood
and salted my own earth,
maybe if I let my self-loathing
eat away my whole self,
the parts left
would be good enough
to raise you.

My son,
I hope you hear this,
Whenever you close your eyes and listen.
I hope you start the long process of forgiving me
Before you learn to hate me.

My dear son,
I will say this
Every time you ask me to,
But I will never say this enough.
Your Daddy loves you very much.

Bryan Erickson, Class of 2015

Bryan Erickson is a junior attending Harvard University, and a
California-born lover of chocolate, small animals, and 80's action
movies.

ARE YOU STILL HEARING VOICES, BY AWAIS HUSSAIN

Do you know why you're here?
Not really, no.

How are you feeling?
Tired. All the time.
I came to you with a physical illness,
Probably something that ends in sclerosis,
My hands keep hurting, and my throats constricted,
This rash is still there, I can sometimes feel it
My fingers keep falling off and my head's lopsided,
And how do you explain this protruding vein in my left eyelid,
I came here today with a physical illness, and yet you keep talking to me
bout this mental …

How are you sleeping?
I sleep standing up in case I dream I'm free falling,
so I can wake up in time and catch with myself,
I make my heart skip a beat and then use it to tell time,
And it's been ticking at a rate that's hard to keep up with
I'll drop a hammer and feather from a leaning tower,
And I might let you choose which one to sit beneath.

How is your social life?
I answer emails with text messages,
Phone calls with retweets,
Snap chat pics of hand written letters,
For you to listen to the next time that we meet in person
See, I'm usually not so shy to begin communicating but,
Your social awkwardness makes you a little intimidating,

Have you been getting out of the house?
I know I'm flying,
But I don't know whether I should be gliding or flapping,
I'm in an ocean, am I floating or kicking,
I can't tell where the ground is, cos I'm high on risperidone pills,
And though your voice sounds heavy I feel real light, headed,
Weigh myself down with these lead balloons so I sink to the surface,
See, I'm trying to fly with my feet on the ground and my head in the
clouds,
I've been poking for a while to figure out where solid earth,
But when I tell you to brace yourself, for I will better the human race,
You give me an Archimedian space to stand - between a rock and a hard
place

Are you still hearing voices?
See we can all fabricate beauty in a whole host of places,

Like how the sun rises each day at just the perfect time,
The unmatched natural wonder of bees in a hive
Don't think I don't hear what you say about me,
Don't think I can't read what you write about me,
And I see through that fake smile to that evil eye,
See I too can leave the bait out, and get you fishhooked on that reel,
And when it rips through your cheek, I'll make you smile through your teeth,
Scribble with invisible ink on transparent toilet paper,
To leave your house looking like it got TP'd by a shy schoolboy who's afraid of committing visible sin
If you've got daggers drawn, I can hold knives too,

How is your appetite?
I know they say I ought to be more careful around you,
But know I can tiptoe and dig my heels in at the same time,
See I've been walking around on eggshells on land mines,
And I invite you to come closer but this field is mine,
Now you might be inclined to erect a zip line,
But can I suggest instead that you go for a tight rope,
Cos I assure you if you leave just one toe out of line,
You might just fall into my reality.

Awais Hussain, Class of 2015

Awais is a physics and philosophy major with a calendar full of colors.

AFTER PARTY

this. is. how. we. do. it.

thank you for walking the line with us,

we hope you found a safety net in these arms.

you don't have to end here,

but you should probably close this book so you can finally sleep.

you've had a fantastic night,

take the morning to write.